THE EXQUISITE PAIN
OF FLOWERING

THE EXQUISITE PAIN OF FLOWERING

MICHELANDE RIDORÉ

The Poetic Method Publishing

The Poetic Method Publishing, 2021

ISBN/SKU 978-0-578-91841-9
eISBN 978-0-578-91842-6

Cover design by Wailoon Chan

The Poetic Method Publishing
an imprint of The Poetic Method, LLC

Through YHWH all things are possible.

To my father, my inspiration, muse, and drill
sergeant all-in-one.

To my mother who defined love for me through
her daily actions.

To my brother who taught me laughter can
brighten up any dark room.

To myself for never giving up.

Contents

I

Seedling

Love Bombing

On your third date, he will say,
"I adore you so."
Ask him, "What is my last name?"

Gaslighting

I can't recall where the lines on your face end and begin,
even though it hasn't been that long.
So, reluctantly, I reflect on routines.

One thousand nine hundred twelve days seem erasable,
but my stomach flips and twists remembering the
fragmenting

weight of lies in between the mechanistic rituals
of a quietly maddening symbiosis.
I know the sky is blue! I remember climbing into my bed, as usual,

on the left side in my new apartment
waking up to the smell of only my shampoo on the other pillow,
while remaining bewildered in motion, I fly

or fight the memories lost between collegiate achievements
and last night's Thai food. I am convinced by fantasies that maybe you
were
never here.

But then why is your absence so intrusive?

Mr. Saboteur

It was a Sunday in October, rainy, yet full of wonder
and as I ached to surrender, you'd tune your guitar.
You'd play chords on my heartstrings—
a haiku you'd serenade, so I always asked for more.
Met with silence, your duper's delight,
so convincing an atonement.
By Monday, drowned in pink clouds, you'd resolved to turn
over the leaves in the Shenandoah, my hope, you yearn
to buy me all the things you'd thought would arrest my tears
to cover the wounds that leave trails by red maples.
We shared starry-eyed visions in the places we've reconciled,
but by Wednesday, you have vanished, seeing her shadows at my side.
And I am muted, while I watch you play the same chords
asking me for recompense during Saturday's remorse.
I waited through dusk's despair,
while you tuned your guitar
so, you can play chords on my heartstrings
while I wonder on a rainy Sunday...

Hide and Seek

You handed me your promises and pleas
and asked me to safeguard the lot for an unknown day and time.
But I'd already dreamt of tomorrow
knowing you'd unravel memories.
You asked me to find you in these lyrics and melodies
of effusive songwriters who have more depth and tune than you.
It isn't longing that keeps me searching on city streets
for the truth, you kept hidden from me,
while you cried in bottles instead.
I've packed up bags and closed our doors more and more with ease
for the chaos that we created, compromises we abated—
a game we play when I run away you come seeking me.
Futures on a platter, you'd suspected you'd found easy prey.
I'll admit my life's stalling has become a skill, my mastery,
but I'm no longer standing behind closed doors waiting for
you to make promises and pleas.
I've already dreamt of tomorrow
knowing I'll make lasting memories.

Absurdities and Soliloquies

A recurring dream.
A repeated scene.
A tapestry of fragmented stories
fill the spaces in our dialogue.
Relating and not relating,
we're engulfed by expectations
on the soapbox of truth deferred.
We tell jokes with embellished punchlines
while scanning each other through the blurred lenses of shame
because quiet authenticity is
a jasper, a wallflower in a sea of charismatic diamonds.
But isolation builds an excessive debt
while we remain unrecognizable.
We cannot fit wholeheartedly
when we do not share our whole hearts.

Patriarchy

Predators come in as chameleons,
civil servants staring while ripping dignity like cloth,
brainwashing us into compliance, a system built to condemn.
Repeatedly we fail to see the patterns within us hidden
that there are stolen birthrights of men taken from women.
And we pass these inheritances down,
reminding our daughters to cross their legs when they sit on the
sidelines.
while we praise our sons for the conquests that leave other girls
undone.

Cancel Culture

We perpetuate conditioned adopted identity
as we are impressionable,
like sheep.
Flocked by identical circumstances—
our great grandfathers, grandfathers, and fathers
are absent so wolves in plain sight seek out the straying.
They pass on ideology to seal the fates
of their sons and grandsons.
The feeble surrender substituting one evil
for another.
In the name of our equality, predators assemble us.
We yield our freedom in our exile.
But they built these fences to keep us from
grazing on the other side.
Because wolves despise our prosperity and our brazen unwillingness
to queue
when we find the Good Shepherd
and the path outside the madness of the pen.

To Be Completely Honest

Months later,
I'm still discovering missing pieces of my timeline,
my truths,
my memories.
I thought I could be honest about my story
without pouring tears into tissues
that never asked to hold these burdens,
my shaken faith,
the lessons I'll smile at someday.
I thought someday was yesterday
when the hours stretched themselves to the corners of my smile,
but today confusion is still intruding,
taking advantage of more days than I offered,
flotsam floating down more miles than the James.

Encrypted Currency

The pat on the back,
the atta-girl,
a yardstick when roads fork.
What would they ask me to do, that is,
what wouldn't end in disapproving glances,
the earsplitting silence?
Could I still their heart?
Dry the sweat off their brows
with a covering of my weighted blanket?
My reluctant yes,
while I build shrines of all the parts of me into a whole person
walking by my side.
Slide into a double life,
the 'mes' I've spent decades stuffing into one
bright pink pocket-sized
mace dispenser.
It's the wall between me
and male fragility when
"I have a boyfriend"
can't always protect me from your retaliation,

your rage,
and your indignation
because some good girls were never taught how to say no
without fearing the
weight of others' unraveling shame.
Especially not to our authorities,
our religious leaders,
our healers,
our policemen—
positioned to build,
to guide,
to heal,
to protect,
and to serve us—
all the while never actually seeing us.

Indignant

Peacekeeping is a chokehold with my own hands.
They are calloused from years of practice.
My anger manifests in bursts of rage or tears.

But there is a still, quiet voice,
a stranger I've walked past many times,
a greeting I've delayed

holding back the dormant wolves I fear may consume me.
Yet, I am much too hungry now!
Watch my releasing while you quiver at my fire.

Dandy

You removed one mask.
Underneath you'd already fastened another,
and another.
Which one are you?
Are you a magician? No, a phantom?
You changed appearances like a ghost,
Depending on your mood and your present host.
Lover, philanderer, hero, abuser,
weaponizing information
terrorizing psyche with emotion.
You spun webs, that is, the tears you shed
while you devoured me
And it would have been an unending cycle, but
for that moment:
filled only with heartbeats and
scrambling silence.
Sitting there with the weight of my denial
abruptly falling from my shoulders like a rucksack at journey's
end.
I saw you.

Mask slipped—in the hypnotic revelations of intuition—
the only serum that's ever worked.
You said nothing.
And that is how I knew
that I never knew you
that you will never know me,
except for the nostalgia of fading memories,
your future tales,
your remaining spoils.
And you will only be the disguises I pray to never see.

Whispers at Dusk

Have I spent my lifetime building
security through learned comforts?
All the while remaining lacking; wanting.
The illusion is palatable.
I practiced rituals for years with an army of enablers
until the day I was shaken awake sitting in my car
outside my home with no memory of how I made it there.

Had I spent the day walking in endless queues
up and down escalators through
sanitized corridors, freshly waxed tile floors,
staring at grey cubicle walls and
outdated calendars with quotes?

There is nothing profound about being a slave to luxuries
I was conditioned to desire.
But there is irony in my dreaming of the very solution,
and entertaining ways my visions may fail.

White Knuckling

He comes always.
Especially during extreme climates
at the striking of the eleventh hour
carrying freedom's timely mercy.
Torn from the reigns of my hands
I bite my nails
and chew on the edges of swollen palms.
Try to divert a misguided discipline to control
mysterious perpetuated dimensions of compulsions.
Simultaneously hating the very desires that elude me.
Embracing despair only when
I confess with the metal breastplate of faith:
I wasn't meant to do this alone.

Shadow Self

One day, helpless and spent, having suffered my last double bind,
with a crochet hook and flesh, I fashion an overcoat so thick, it is
impenetrable.

Just like my body.
I feed it perfectionism, lies, and wear a poker face
until it hardens a mask so indistinguishable, I walk right past myself.
I tell the world *I prefer to walk alone,*
all the while feeling rejected.

But my shame is a cinderblock hanging from my lowered head.
All I see is the pavement that leads to the familiar comforts of an
empty room.

In silence, I seek an answer:
"How can I remain hidden and still love myself,
and still, be loved by others?"

I find
I've been walking

for miles
at the same
two feet
of space.

When the weight on my chest molds me to the floor,
I tear through threads—
loosen layers and falsehoods of a battered virago.
Imperfectly lovely.
Ready.

Kõan

When he is finally gone
my body doesn't know he didn't die.
It writhes, drains, contests, and blames.
My hands don't know it will no longer hold his.
My brain flashes images of me in distress, in joy,
and leaves me there to resolve my ruptured ideology—
that he was everything he said he wasn't
and none of the things he promised he was.

II

Budding

Autumn

Falling
in the cold nips at your neck,
your ankles, and kisses
your nose inflamed.
Scents of cinnamon and ginger spice.
A visual cacophony of green leaves
exhaling into orange and yellow.
Autumn is the yin to Spring—
an ever-evolving breathtaking decay—
resting, regenerating, and empowering.

Prayer for a Prideful Heart

Every time I think I've won,
figured out the perfect formula,
I am broken.
Again, and again, I'm emboldened
to put my fractured pieces together again
only to be lost in—déjà vu.

What day is it?
I've shattered so much only dust remains.
These tiny grains.
Every time I caulk the final piece,
You hold up a mirror to my dis-*ease*
and I'm right back where I started.

Too afraid to drop everything,
but it's my plans You boldly thwart
to show me my efforts were never sought.
All I ask is that You heal the exhaustion,
the searching, the running, and the rumination.
I've logged endless hours outside you.

But I'm praying your promises remain everlasting,
that my heart is true to your molding,
And that I live to fulfill Your purpose.

Apple

Some people will ask You to measure Your magnitude.
To which You'll furrow Your 'brows'
Because You know You are an apple and a seed—
the ending and beginning of everything.

I would rather swallow You whole than count You.
In my nooks and crannies, You grow roots
that stretch me from limb to limb
until Your branches give way and You birth more fruit.

New Moon

Take off your make-up and heels,
put down your sword and your shield,
you never needed them anyway.
Move in your direction, that's the right way.
May your dresses always let you twirl
while your feet spin your whole world.
The closer you are to the ground,
the better they will hear your sounds.
Let out that earthly, feminine growl,
it's the new moon after all.
Here they come to find you humming
sweetly, now you can join in honeyed harmony.

Authenticity

Don't strategize, hold space.
Adjust to life's cyclical pace.
Call it by its name.
Always tell your heart's tale.
Patience allows you to see energy.
Speak your words then, a soft synchronicity.
Harmony is sound waves matching light ones,
that is when your words match your actions.
This allows you to see truth echoing in your ear.
You will then feel your path, follow it without fear.

UFOs

The route to feeling grounded lies in following your intuition.
It lives lower in my body between my gut and my feet.
If I feel conflicted, it's because I am being led astray by thoughts—
these live higher up, so high they feel like UFOs:
Uninvited Foreign Obstructions.
When I feel split,
I listen to things that pull me to the Earth.

A Connecting Energy

I am abandoning should-haves.
They are destructive, splitting
us in twos and threes.
But we were built to be whole.
Between us, there is nothing, but
energy.
You are miles away and as you stroke
your cheeks, mine are rouged.

Rebirth

If reincarnation is real,
I hope we're reborn as two tricolor mountain pups—
Who'll never ask, "Am I good enough?"
Or amber-beaked waterfowl,
Who haven't been tamed by tales of Icarus?
Or dandelions growing with each new sunrise
As they form cracks in renewed pavement.
So, that I never have to play shame's warped records
Over the sounds of you whispering, "I love you."

Unlocked

I am waving a white flag, high.
I know You can see it fly.
People say right timing is key.
I think I was locked, and somehow now we're fitting.
So, I will surrender to every turn.
I don't know what will come tomorrow morn,
but with every ray of light that You shine on me,
I'm a cymbidium budding, my layers You set free.

Exhale

There are cotton balls in my throat.
Behind them, sourness burns
through layers of flesh down to my chest.
Swallowing an anvil that sits on my lungs.
I am immobilized.
Your expectations are a marathon I've spent years running,
stalling the finish line of disappointment.
We cannot call it loving when it isn't freeing,
when it is your will that binds me.
Kiss my wings as I fly away!

III

Flowering

Interior Designs

Some things belong in our living room,
a table for dinners,
a mantle for portraits
a couch that comfortably seats just enough of
The people who ask you,
    "How's your heart?"
    "How's your father's back?"

The people who shed tears after discovering
they've missed your moments,
but remind you that even when the lights are off
someone else's heartbeat matches your own.

It's where solitude is being wrapped
in the softest blanket in the house
so, you can inhale and exhale
while tears pool in the crevices of collar bones
until you see that you're still breathing,
and that nothing, no matter how bleak, is insurmountable.

There is joy in the sigh that comes from accepting
that certain things come into our homes to stay.
While others run in through the back patio,
and out the front door like a bandit being chased away.

An Expanding Spectrum

It never occurred to me that love could look
different than I expected.
Books and movies will have us believe that love is red—
consuming and stimulating.

But I have felt love as the color blue—
the hottest part of a flame,
and as the color green—
as earthly and sturdy as a Sequoia Redwood.

But it wasn't until I abandoned
all preconceptions of what it should be,
did I find love is white:
so soft you can miss it looking for it elsewhere.
It is made up of the entire spectrum;
it doesn't absorb us; it only mirrors us.

Faith

Though it has an air of confidence, it is not clairvoyance.
Like an unwavering curiosity, it is gifted through waiting,
through obstacle courses,
delayed rewards,
a delivery of unexpected virtue.
Smiling, while knowing nothing,
and having no timeline for its arrival.
A growing intuition at every part of your journey.
You will always find yourself.
You will never lose, be lost, or be without Him.

Boundless

What if we lived in a world without labels
in which we weren't defined within strict boundaries?
We create lines to instruct,
but the young mind is
b o u n d l e s s
It doesn't know the word blue.
It doesn't call heartache depression. It isn't limited by
horizontal
time.
Aren't we all one thought, one extra voice away
from lunacy?
from bigotry?
If so, we are also one moment away
from understanding,
acceptance,
contradiction,
unconditional love.

Catch Up

You are tangy, yet sweet, often maroon and saucy.
I don't want you to think that you make me complete,
but several times a day,
I find things lacking without you.
A bland and lifeless parody,
of often perfected staples;
sitting, waiting, bitten and bruised;
left behind for ridicule.
Oh, how they take you for granted—
Those highbrows, only browse high
For far superior versions of you
that never quite fit with true American fare.
But the masses all yearn for you eventually,
as you are tied to the eternal and universal nostalgia
of summer nights in backyard barbeques filling the air,
so thick, the neighborhood boys can almost chew it as it lingers.
You are the first innings, many beginnings, in roaring crowds;
Yet also quiet, late-night dinners for 4, or for one.
Sitting near plates filled with comfort,
And just good old-fashioned French fries.

A Calling Before Dawn

At 12:25 am,
phrases thirsting to be written flood my head and I'm awakened
from the nightmare of forgetting perfectly juxtaposed diction
loosening shadows from their hiding places,
the dark corners of my room where silence goes to scream.

Trombones in organ chambers grow louder
as they echo in a hardened heart.

But it cannot be ignored when they
invade others' dreams as they become
witnesses to the calling, and pulling,
while I pour out the contents of my being in
endless ink I cannot stop
my pen accompanies the metaphors my body seeks to shout!

You Can't Fix Me

You can't fix my mad.
You can't fix my sad.

But I've spent my life diagnosing boys who echo your sorrow,
pained and artfully disguised by your fortitude.
You stand, overcoming a lost attachment to Attalea,
a disrupted forestation in a rapidly decaying country,
though you've never appeared stunted to me.
Instead, you transformed into an artisan,
chiseling away at my subtle defects,
often in a battle,
you with woodworking instruments,
and I with my fraud—
a lifelong sin you've spent your life diagnosing
while rescuing me from boys
who dig shallow graves for the pieces of me they thieve,
and the measures I've taken to relinquish them.
I am hollow now.
I've unearthed the roots of our tree.
Generations of branching and climbing vines far-reaching,

some brittle, some twined.
With our limbs, we've built foundations for flowering.
Our barks repair from the harshness of sun and frost,

But I have learned that I cannot fix your mad.
And though I have labored, I cannot fix your sad.

My Morning Song

My morning song begins
like cool oil cascading down my crown.
A groundhog's day reset of seasons.
A song is heard.
It sounds like an answer to a lifetime of questions,
like unlabored breathing after anaphylaxis,
like splashes of rhythmic pulses and pedaling in a vast sea.
Fierce choruses of waves quietly blend into verse.
Wavy notes tirelessly rise and fall composing lyrics to 'Healing.'

Healing

My chest is heavy and cloaked
with shallow breathing, faint and queasy.
Though I'm not one to lay idle when poked,
still, I sit, I sit silently shrill.
Governed by pressure, to blame, shame, and punish you,
I'm coaxing deliverance.
The lip of the wave falls,
and a single tear breaks from the pack.
I'm betrayed by my nerves, who knew before I did
the agony of pride and fear—
a peculiar blessing that taught me
to honor the path on which YHWH has placed you,
while honoring the one He's given me.

In My Wildest Dreams

All the blemishes,
the scars,
and hollowed parts of me
have lightened,
and filled with
the unseen,
the yet experienced,
the hallelujah,
the exhale,
the drawn-out schedule-less Saturday morning slumber
on a sunny summer day that beckons from the window
of a house on a hill filled with little running feet
who never have to worry about dinner time,
or when dad's coming home because there is no doubting
love's true nature,
the reliability of safety,
of wholeness, of enduring presence.

Refuge

I quaked at each syllable when
I heard your voice the first time when
it'd seemed I'd heard it before when
you sat across me looking like kin, but a stranger then
I couldn't reconcile why, at that moment, then,
I'd wished I was the drop of water then
sliding down my water glass sinking in
the remaining sip, a world away from this moment in
my life when I'd never before been so adamant in
shying away from your eyes fearing I'd be hypnotized in
believing that all this is part of our story and
those times I walked away I was actually running to you and
you strengthened my faith before I knew I needed it and
you daringly poured yourself in
to my dreams, the spaces between, in
today and tomorrow, all I can recall in
daylight is a moment some time from now when
I'm with you by a dock in our old city when
you ask me again if you can watch over me, when
all I say this time is 'I'm ready, I wish I'd always been.'

Enough

Perfection is a battle.

A war with self.

How could I believe I could attain it through diligence and pride alone?

There are curves on my body I spent decades trying to erase.

A mysteriously placed masterpiece of immeasurable precision.

How could I win a fight that You've already won?

Who am I to make adjustments to gold?

Or buy into the lies that I was not wondrously made?

Perception of purpose is only perfected in You.

Bring Me to My Mountain

Hello old friend,
forgive my absence.

It's been a winding
journey back to you in your lined walls.

Very stable and constant as you are.
You never ask for more, but your boundaries are clear.

You sit there waiting,
as lovely as I've ever seen.

Shall we do this dance,
let you lead me by my heart?

Through the dark lines and curves of broken
penmanship that has evolved with age.

Subtle flows of inspiration
begin to flood each time I return to these pages.

What you've been asking for
this whole time is a commitment to my purpose.

How embarrassingly simple?

And here we are again
shifting onto another page.

You are a canvas of solitude,
your blank space—

An invitation for authenticity,
of love absolute,
and emotions thought, and wisdom in abundance.

The physical manifestation of staircase wit.
Two moments too late—
an abridged version of analysis paralysis
for the masses.

This is the process of life and death,
the many moments in between,
that grow our understanding,
our courage in loving us,
and, most importantly,
our faith when facing the mountain of loving others well.

All Along

While the choir sings
'We never liked him anyway'
I place my hand upon my chest
feel the pitter-patter
grind my teeth a little louder
above the tingling in my left breast
a stinging imperceptible
until I'd quieted the wheezing in my lungs
sang a flurry of worship songs
so, He'd know my heart was grateful
that through the lengthened days and sleepless nights
He'd been there all along.

As a public health advocate, Michelande Ridoré has previously been published in the Official Journal of the American Academy of Pediatrics, American Journal of Perinatology, Vaccine, BMC Infectious Diseases as well as several other peer-reviewed medical journals. A long-time writer and poet, *The Exquisite Pain of Flowering* is her first published collection of poetry. She currently serves as the quality manager for the Children's Hospital of Richmond in Richmond, Virginia where she resides.